LITTLE BABY JESUS

BY
ARINZE KENE

**First produced at Oval House Theatre, London,
on Wednesday 25 May**

LITTLE BABY JESUS · BY ARINZE KENE

Cast in order of appearance

KEHINDE	Fiston Barek
JOANNE	Seroca Davis
RUGRAT	Akemnji Ndifernyen

Creative Team

Director	Ché Walker
Production Designer	Chris Gylee
Lighting Designer	Arnim Friess
Composer & Sound Designer	Richard Hammarton
Costume Supervisor	Bianca Ward
Assistant Designer	Philippa Thomas
Scenic Artist	Katie Jamieson
Assistant Director	Kemi David
Production Manager	Bernd Fauler
Deputy Stage Manager	Suu Wernham
Assistant Stage Manager	Sylvia Darkwa-Ohemeng
Publicity Design	Lulu Kitololo (asilia)

Production Acknowledgements

Claire Birch at English Touring Theatre, Fay Davies, Leanne Dunstan, Bayo Gbadanosi, Barbara Gordon, Shia Miller, Didi Mokwe, Stef O'Driscoll, Michelle Thompson, CCMS cleaning services, Smiths Florists, Sparks Hire, 33% Festival

Season Producers

Oval House is a local theatre for an international city dedicated to staging brave new work by artists who are too uncompromising for the mainstream. We present theatre that is relevant to the UK's cosmopolitan capital and, reflecting contemporary London, Oval's programme is increasingly international in focus. We champion stories that you will not hear anywhere else and invest in exploration and development, inspiring artists to challenge themselves to become the world-class theatre makers of tomorrow.

BEcreative develops and presents theatre in London, the UK, and abroad – making international theatre for a local audience. Led by Creative Director, Ben Evans, BEcreative offers bespoke artistic and managerial support to risk-taking theatre makers challenging the mainstream.

Little Baby Jesus is supported by the **English Touring Theatre**. As one of England's foremost theatre companies, ETT creates theatre of outstanding quality, imagination and ambition that is both emotionally and intellectually engaging. The company works with the country's leading directors and practitioners to produce artistically ambitious theatre that is vigorous, popular and challenging, as well as confident and forward-looking.

Cast

Fiston Barek – KEHINDE
Fiston made his professional debut at the National Theatre where he played Joseph in *Love the Sinner*. He has since played Joshua in *Doctors*. Credits from ALRA include: Rob in *Children in Wartime*, Sonny in *Rise*, Jim in *Gut Girls*, Narcissus in *Tales from Ovid*, Quentin in *After the Fall*, Claudio in *Much Ado About Nothing* and Romeo in *Romeo and Juliet*.

Seroca Davis – JOANNE
Seroca's most recent theatre credit was for the Royal Court's production of *random*, a one-woman show directed by Sasha Wares. Theatre: *Love's Labour's Lost* (Shakespeare's Globe and US tour), *We the People* (Shakespeare's Globe); *Don Juan in Soho* (with Rhys Ifans at the Donmar Warehouse); *93.2fm* (Royal Court); *Master Juba Project* (Albany); *Little Sweet Thing* (UK tour). Television: *Dr Who, Holby City, Criminal Justice, That Mitchell and Webb Look, Horne & Corden, The Bill, Prime Suspect 7, More Than Love, Comin Atcha, Homework High, Daylight Robbery II, Snap, Understanding Electricity*. Film: *Innocent Pink, London Birds Can't Fly, Kidscape, Picture Power*. Radio: Hands, *Gone, Starmass*. Seroca won the 2005 Manchester Evening News Award for Best Actress for her performance in *Little Sweet Thing*.

Akemnji Ndifernyan – RUGRAT
Theatre: *The Golden Hour* (Almeida); *Shoot/Get Treasure/Repeat, Chatroom/Citizenship, The History Boys* (National Theatre). Television: *Leonardo* (Mammoth/BBC); *Law & Order* (UK, Kudos/ITV); *Bo and the Spirit World, MI High, Casualty, Broken News, The Everglades, Doctors, The Crouches* (BBC). Film: *Incubus* (Junction Film); *Life 'n' Lyrics* (Lyric Films Ltd); *Snowman* (Dogma; Ideal World); *Out of Control* (BBC Films).

Creative Team

Arinze Kene – Writer
Arinze Kene was born in Lagos, Nigeria and in 1991 his family moved to London. He trained and still works as an actor as well as working as a writer-director. Arinze is currently writing for BBC3's third series of *E20*. He wrote *Woosah* for The Old Vic's 24Hour Plays, 2010 and Defined by Design for The Old Vic/ Time Warner's Ignite, 2010. His play *Estate Walls* was first performed as a reading at the Theatre Royal Stratford East in December 2008, followed by a rehearsed reading at the Young Vic Theatre in October 2009 and a full production at Oval House Theatre in September 2010, directed by Ché Walker. Arinze wrote *Us & Them* for The Bush Theatre and Nabokov's Wrap-around, 2010. He was a member of the Young Writers' Programme at the Royal Court Theatre, was invited onto the Soho Theatre's Young Writers Group and is now part of Soho Theatre HUB writer's programme. He was shortlisted for Off West End's 2010's 'Adopt a Playwright Award' and the 2009 Alfred Fagon Award. Arinze won an Off West End Theatre Award for Most Promising Playwright in 2011. *Little Baby Jesus* is recipient of the Mark Marvin Rent Subsidy Award, as part of the Peter Brook Empty Space Awards.

Sarah Crompton – Production Assistant
Sarah is a freelance producer, currently working in London and Cambridge. She has been working on the stage and behind the scenes since she was young, but moved into producing theatre three years ago. Since then she has worked with Gecko Theatre Company (Assistant Producer of *The Overcoat*), State of Emergency Dance Company (Co-tour Manager), Shatterbox (Producer of *Fair Trade*), and is currently producing *Romeo and Juliet* for Night Light Theatre Company in Cambridge.

Sylvia Darkwa-Ohemeng – Assistant Stage Manager
Sylvia is in her third year currently studying at Rose Bruford College doing a BA (Hons) degree in Stage Management. She has been freelancing at Oval House since August, working on shows including *Estate Walls* by Arinze Kene. She was also heavily

involved in the 33% London Festival working as one of the stage managers. She has also worked at the Cochrane Theatre, Unicorn Theatre and the Playhouse Theatre, Embankment, and festivals like SouthWestFest. She is hoping to increase her skills within the profession and travel within her career.

Kemi David – Assistant Director
Kemi is an aspiring director with interests spanning across both film and theatre. Stage credits include: *Black Man's Monologue* by Ola Masha (Battersea Arts Centre); *Who Let the Dogs Out, 10 Naira* (ATC/Soho) and *364* by Lashana Lynch (Lyric Hammersmith). She is currently developing a short film project.

Arnim Friess – Lighting Designer
Arnim trained and worked as a photographer and audio-visual media designer in his native Germany, before moving to the UK to study Scenography, receiving an MA at Birmingham Institute of Art and Design. He is the founder member of Pixelbox Ltd, which specialises in designing dynamic performance environments, blending media like lighting, slide and video projection, animation, film-making and graphic design. Recent designs include: *Ghosts in the Walls* (RSC); *The Rememberers* (Birmingham REP and Apples&Snakes); *We love You City* (Talking Birds at Belgrade). Past designs include: science-fiction opera *The Pitchshifter* for leading Dutch contemporary music ensemble Insomnia, award-winning *Rumblefish*, bricks-in-space spectacle *Life on Mars* (Legolands worldwide).

Bernd Fauler – Production Manager
Bernd enjoys working as a freelance production manager on a variety of projects, including contemporary performance/live art, theatre and dance as well as outdoor performances. Credits include: Sacred 2009/2010, a Season of Contemporary Performance (Chelsea); *That's the Way to Do It* (Red Herring Productions); *Access All Areas* (Live Art Development Agency); *Gross Indecency* (Duckie); *Hurts Given And Received / Slowly* (Howard Barker Season 2010 at Riverside Studios); *Soulplay, Kate Flatt Projects, Where's My Desi Soulmate, It Ain't All Bollywood, Meri Christmas, The Deranged Marriage* (Rifco Arts).

Chris Gylee – Designer

Chris trained at Bristol Old Vic Theatre School and was a selected designer on Cheek by Jowl's inaugural Young Director/ Designer programme. For Shakespeare at the Tobacco Factory, Bristol, he has designed *Hamlet*, *The Taming of the Shrew*, *Othello* and *Much Ado About Nothing*. Other plays include: *Henry V* (Southwark Playhouse); *Colörs*, *Tattoo* (Company of Angels); *Grimms – The Final Chapter* (Trafalgar Studios); *Not Knowing Who We Are* (Blue Elephant); and designs for Arts Ed, Theatre503, Bristol Old Vic, and the Jermyn Street Theatre. Site-specific designs: *Fanshen* (Theatre Delicatessen); *Shooting Rats* (fanSHEN); *Oliver Twist* (the egg). Chris is an associate designer with Fairground for whom he designed *The Red Man*, *Out of Touch* and *Bonnie & Clyde*. Chris's work as an illustrator and artist includes performance collaborations with Bristol Ferment.

Richard Hammarton – Composer & Sound Designer

Theatre includes *Dr Faustus* (Manchester Royal Exchange); *Speaking in Tongues* (Duke of Yorks); *Ghosts* (Duchess); *People at Sea*, *The Real Thing*, *Arsenic and Old Lace*, *Les Liaisons Dangereuses*, *The Constant Wife* (Salisbury Playhouse); *Pride and Prejudice* (Bath Theatre Royal and national tour); *The Mountaintop* (Trafalgar 1/Theatre503); *Breakfast With Mugabe* (Bath Ustinov); *Some Kind of Bliss*, *World's End*, *Hello and Goodbye* (Trafalgar Studios); *The Rise and Fall of Little Voice* (Harrogate). TV/Film composition includes: *Agatha Christie's Marple* (Series 3, 4), *The Secret of Chimneys* (ITV); *Wipeout* (children's drama); *Sex 'n' Death* (BBC); *Rajan and his Evil Hypnotist* (Channel 4). TV/Film orchestration includes *Primeval*, *Jericho*, *Agatha Christie's Marple* (series 1 & 2); *The Nine Lives of Tomas Katz* (UK Feature Films).

Philippa Thomas – Assistant Designer

After studying illustration at Edinburgh College of Art, Philippa decided to make the move into the world of performance with a Masters in Set and Costume Design at the Bristol Old Vic Theatre School two years ago. Since graduating she has enjoyed working with a variety of companies and practitioners in theatre, film, festival and events. She is living and working in Bristol and is currently happy to find herself at Oval House Theatre for the first time.

Bianca Ward – Costume Supervisor
Bianca Ward trained at Bristol Old Vic Theatre School. Previously having studied Textiles at Central Saint Martins, she has now honed her skills to incorporate textiles into her costume practice. Recently she has co-designed costumes and supervised a show with Edward Sharpe and the Magnetic Zeros at the Old Vic Tunnels. At Christmas she supervised *Pinocchio* at the Tobacco Factory, Bristol, and has made for and assisted the recent Shakespeare season there. As well as supervising this year she also made costumes for BBC period drama *32 Brinkburn Street* and for *Thriller the Musical*.

Ché Walker – Director
Directing: Theatre – *Been So Long the Musical* (Young Vic/ English Touring Theatre); *The Last Days of Judas Iscariot*, *The Lights* (Arts Ed); *A Mouthful of Birds*, *Balm in Gilead* (RADA); *A Flea in Her Ear*, *Hot L Baltimore* (Corbett); *Etta Jenks*, *Achidi J's Final Hours* (Finborough); *The Big Nickel* (National Youth Theatre and Soho). Film shorts – *Crocodile in snow*, *Crazy Love*, *At It Again*. Acting: *Othello* (Shakespeare's Globe); *Love's Labour's Lost* (Shakespeare's Globe/National Theatre of Korea); *Etta Jenks* (Finborough). Writing: *Been So Long the Musical* (Young Vic); *The Frontline* (Shakespeare's Globe); *Crazy Love* (Paines Plough/ Orán Mòr).

Suu Wernham – Deputy Stage Manager
Suu began her career working as a sound engineer at the London Palladium on *The King and I*, *Barnum* and *Singing in the Rain*. Following this she spent several years with the Royal Shakespeare Company at the Barbican before returning to stage management and touring with companies such as the Reduced Shakespeare Company, the Young Vic, and English Touring Theatre. Having recently spent time in the USA developing projects with theatre companies and musicians, she hopes to continue this work in the future.

Oval House

Since the 1960s, Oval House Theatre has been a pioneering supporter of queer, feminist and ethnically diverse performance work and we remain committed to exploding preconceptions of what theatre is and can be.

Today, Oval House is a local theatre for an international city dedicated to staging brave new work by artists who are too uncompromising for the mainstream. We work with the most exciting companies from London, the UK and beyond to present theatre that is relevant to the UK's cosmopolitan capital.

We champion stories that you will not hear anywhere else and invest in exploration and development, inspiring artists to challenge themselves to become the world-class theatre-makers of tomorrow.

Autumn 2011 at Oval House Theatre

We open with an explosion of Latin American culture: the return of CASA Festival brings us the very best of contemporary hispanic performance.

Autumn at Oval House Theatre sees a Lady-Led season filled with the bold new voices of some of the UK's most exciting female theatre-makers.

We present two incredible new plays by two distinctive playwrights. Stacey Gregg's *Lagan* and Shireen Mula's *Same Same* subvert familiar theatrical forms to tell compelling stories of longing and belonging.

Stella Duffy returns to Oval House with Shaky Isles and their story of sea monsters in the London sewers: Taniwha Thames.

Following a sellout work in progress showing as part of our transgressions season, we welcome back Mars.tarrab with *Tomboy Blues: The Theory of Disappointment* for more disappointment, more theories and more culottes.

See you in the Autumn.

Oval House Theatre
52-54 Kennington Oval
London
SE11 5SW

Tel: 020 7582 0080
Fax: 020 7820 0990
info@ovalhouse.com
www.ovalhouse.com

Oval House Theatre

Oval House Theatre and the London via Lagos festival gratefully acknowledge financial
support from Arts Council England, Lambeth Arts, London Councils, The Morel
Charitable Trust, The Steele Charitable Trust, The Gibbs Charitable Trust, Unity Theatre
Trust, The 8th Earl of Sandwich Memorial Trust, Grange Farm Trust, the Royal Victoria Hall
Foundation, The Peter Brook Mark Marvin Rent Subsidy Award and Barry Cox.

Photos by: Robert Day and Richard Hubert Smith

surprise • delight • enrich • engage

Under the directorship of Rachel Tackley, ETT presents potent, vivid and vital productions of new and classic plays to audiences far and wide. A powerhouse of touring theatre, ETT works with a rich and varied mix of the country's leading directors, actors and artists to stage thrilling and ambitious theatre that is vigorous, popular and, above all, entertaining.

Supported by
ARTS COUNCIL
ENGLAND

www.ett.org.uk

LITTLE BABY JESUS

Arinze Kene

Characters

RUGRAT, *ex-schoolboy*

JOANNE, *ex-schoolgirl*

KEHINDE, *the boy who never leaves*

Synopsis

*A lyrical triptych of monologues based around the lives of three
distinct school pupils. Each account is a riveting narrative
relaying the exact point that a teenager becomes an adult. They
are written to be appreciated together.*

Set in contemporary inner-city London.

*This text went to press before the end of rehearsals and so may
differ slightly from the play as performed.*

PROLOGUE

KEHINDE. As the world gets better at spinning.

JOANNE. We get dizzy and fall on our rare.

RUGRAT. Some keep falling through the atmosphere.

KEHINDE. Some don't survive past 12:05.

JOANNE. But if you've got *this* – (*Heart.*)

RUGRAT. And if you use *this* – (*Brains.*)

KEHINDE. Then you don't need much or a little bit else.

ONE

Kehinde

(KEHINDE *is sixteen, black. He is mature, very sensible for his age, but there is a sensitivity about him; an innocence.*)

I used to have 'mixed-raced-girl syndrome'. Mixed-race-girl syndrome is the long obsessive phase of over-fancying mixed-race girls. Girls of that lighter complexion. Most guys get it when they're like fourteen, fifteen. My favourite was when that black African or Caribbean skin mixes with that white English or European skin. You get that sun-kissed finish.

At one point. I actually wanted to be mixed-race. I wished for it. I wished my hair wouldn't curl over itself like pepper grains, I wanted it to be bouncy and coolie. But no, broom bristles instead I concluded I was stuck with. I'd gladly have traded this nose for one that was sharper at the end. Shameful, I know. I was so stupid, I got down one time, asked God to forgive me for my sins, to protect my family and to bless me with pink lips. I actually remember going to sleep wishing that I'd wake up with green eyes.

My prayers were obviously ignored and I didn't turn into a mixed-raced boy. And if I were God I would've blanked me for a year just to chastise me for being so ungrateful of this beautiful black skin I was gifted with – Praise God. Believe I had a lot of growing up to do.

Well, I couldn't have grown up all that quick though because next I got a really light-skinned girlfriend. I just couldn't leave the lighties alone. Said, if I couldn't be one, I'd have to represent one – to compensate.

My grandma calls it 'Yellow Fever'. She said it all started around slavery times when white overseers would secretly admire the beauty. I'm sure that back then it was nothing to rape black women. Africa was like the white man's back garden and he did whatever he saw fit with his fruit. She said it's not our fault though, she says something's wrong with us. She always used to say –

(*Nigerian accent.*) *'You African men are magnet for oyinbo pehpeh too much. You de follow-follow and think you are among dem but they will let you know how black you are. IF you trust a white man to build the ceiling above your head, you mustn't complain of neck problems, my child, na your fault be dat!'*

If I bring home a girl who's any bit lighter than me then –

'Ah-Kehinde! It's getting late, your oyinbo friend has to go home. Doesn't she have a home or have her parents split up?'

Cos all white people's parents are divorced according to Grandma.

My older brother, he would sneak girls into the house all the time. When Grandma would go by his room, he'd get the girl to hide down on the side of the bed, on the floor.

Joanne's Prelude

(JOANNE *is a schoolgirl, fifteen years young, mixed-raced,*
fresh-faced, dipped in rudeness and rolled in attitude. She
wears her school uniform and a pink mini-backpack. She is only
young but something about her is profoundly jaded. She is a lot
older than her years.

She stops to stick her chewing gum under a desk.)

JOANNE. When you're born
    You should get
    A manual that says:
    'Okay listen up, you have seventy-five years to be all you
    can be!'

CHORUS. GO!!!!

JOANNE. Rather than wastin' your time, getting caught up with
    things like… religion.

CHORUS. And finance.

JOANNE. And school!

CHORUS. Schooooool!

JOANNE. Flippin' school.

CHORUS. Schooooool dinners.

JOANNE. Oh! Don't EVEN get me started on da food.

CHORUS. It ain't soul food.

JOANNE. And it ain't food for thought.

    It gets all stuck between your cheek and your gums AND it
    slides down your throat too damn slow. No joke. This one
    time, the fucking chips took so long to get to my belly that I
    thought I was gonna choke. Could not breathe. It stopped in
    the middle of my chest and just jammed there. Had to take

three mighty swigs of *IRN-BRU* to wash it down. Oil-drinking simulation. Real talk – next lunchtime I'm boppin' straight out of school gates for a smoke and that's me. I beg a teacher try chat dust to me about smoking in my uniform and see if I don't tiger-punch a dinner lady through her temple to send her staggering for pavement – Real.

But what's worst than school. After school I haunt the 271 bus route for a couple journeys to kill time before I touch the morbidity that is a place I'm forced to call my home. Don't even wanna put my keys in the door more-times but that's the only door I got keys to. Ptshh. It's Mum, innit.

CHORUS. Mum Mum.

JOANNE. Can I switch the telly on?

CHORUS. Mum Mum.

JOANNE. But Mum, I can't sleep.

CHORUS. Mum Mum.

JOANNE. Mum, I'm not being funny…

CHORUS. Mum Mum.

JOANNE. … but can I have my dinner money please?

CHORUS. Mum Mum.

JOANNE. Aaaahh MUM!

CHORUS. Mum Mum.

JOANNE. You're so… you're so dumb!

CHORUS. Mum Mum.

JOANNE. You make me wanna die.

CHORUS. Mum Mum.

JOANNE. THAT'S WHY I'LL NEVER BE A MUM!

I will throw my baby away before she goes through anything you put me through.

(JOANNE, *on her journey to school, 'rocks'* (*customises*) *her school uniform.*

*She rolls up the skirt until it is too short. She pulls her
popsocks up to the knee. Fixes her hair bun to one side.
Buttons down her school shirt to show a bit of cleavage, and
turns the shirt collar out.)*

Joanne

Whenever we had science and we'd do lessons on magnetism,
by the end of the lesson there'd always be a few magnets
missing. At least one of them were in *my* pocket. It's a known
fact that human beings love magnets. No matter how old you
get you still find them fascinating.

When I was younger, primary-school days, I'd carry around
this magnet that I'd stolen from school and on my journey
home I'd see how many things it was attracted to. It killed me
doing that. I'd stick it on the railings, on gates, on the postbox,
drains, lamp posts, doorknobs, cars, telephone box, bus stop,
fences. I think people are like magnets. When we come
together we repel or attract.

Me and my mum are red magnets, so we repelled. Constantly
trying to get away from each other. We hated being out together.
Like… I had to go hospital one time cos I slipped in the shower.
See, most people sing in the shower. I dance. That's how I got
this scar. Slipped and split my head open on a tile. I remember
that day like it was Monday. The water in the shower turned
pink all of a sudden. It didn't hurt until I saw blood.

Had to wait for-eh-ver at A&E. Just me and Mum, in public,
uuh, nuff uncomfortable. Nuff people who came after us were
getting seen to first. That was making Mum vexed. On some
Incredible Hulk flex – anger problems. She's one of those
people, once she gets started, everything, Every Little Thing,
pisses her off. So she's sitting in her chair at one hundred
degrees Fahrenheit – just fuming. She kept telling me to close
my leg –

'Close your leg, girl!'

It's really not that big a deal. I sit with 'em open, so what?
We're not in the 1800's – real talk. If I'm wearing jeans I wanna
feel free to go – (*Opens legs.*) ya get me? I'm there finking –

*'Mum, Mum, I broke my fucking head tonight yeah and you're
obsessing over my open leg. Please. I beg. Get over yourself.
It's not that deep.'*

Didn't actually say that to her though, she would've blasted
another gash up-side my head – real talk.

We got back home and I think she was still upset –

'Joanne, go and wash your blood out the shower curtain.'

She was so nice to me sometimes?

Rugrat's Prelude

(RUGRAT *is a class clown, underachiever, shit-stirrer,
playground loudmouth. He's on the outer of the inner circle.
Hanging with the bad boys but always watching, and
commentating, never getting his hands dirty.*

RUGRAT, *in lunchbreak detention, is indignantly writing lines.
He keeps looking out of the window –*)

RUGRAT. I must not disrupt this class
    I must not disrupt this class
    I must not disrupt this class
    I must not disrupt this class

Ah dis is long! (*Shortcut.*)

I I I I I I I

Must Must Must Must Must Must Must

(CHORUS *join in.*)

Not Not Not Not Not Not Not

Disrupt Disrupt Disrupt Disrupt

This This This This

Class Class Class Class Class Class Class Class Class Class
Class Class

CHORUS. Sometimes

CHORUS. I'm doing it

RUGRAT. Just so you can notice me

CHORUS. Notice me, notice, just so you can notice me –
(*Repeat over and over.*)

RUGRAT (*talking to Mr Taruvangadum, over the* CHORUS).
Oi, sir. Sir! Can I go now?
I'm finished though, look.
Everyone else is outside playing football.
Sir!
But other people were saying it too, why didn't you say
nothing to *them*?
OH MY DAYS! How was it only me though? Jerome!
Jerome said it before me even. Yeah, you *wouldn't* hear him,
would you. You've got selective hearing you know that, sir?
Nah nothing, I said nothing.

(*Flops back down in his chair, crosses his arms.*)

THIS IS SO UNFAIR!

(*Under his breath.*) Ah shut up, man, look at your head.
…Pardon?
Yeah… (*To himself.*) but you never say anything good about
me though, do you? Never say *I* got a bright future ahead of
me.
(*Mumbles.*) Please.
I *said* please!
Thank you.

(RUGRAT *jumps to his feet and races out of the classroom…*

*…reaching the playground just as the ball is blasted over the
fence. Disappointed.*)

Rugrat

Ahh! I flipping hated whenever the ball went over the fence.
And you know who toe-punted it, innit? Babatunde. That guy,
man. When he first come to our school in Year 9, this is no lie –
on his first day he was wearing sandals, blood. Sandals. Man
was like –

'Where you going with those, rude boi?'

Teacher was bussing up, he tried to keep a straight face but it
was the way he just sidestepped into registration; firstly, no one
knows who he is, secondly, man had SANDALS. (*Laughing*.)

I was dead, I died – ah Jerome, Jerome's my boi, innit, Jerome
said something like how –

'Babatunde got those sandals from Jerusalem, rude boi!'

Wooo! That is what sent me. I flung my chair across the room, I
was cry-laughing, rolling on the floor and all sorts –

'Did you rob them sandals off Jesus, fam?'

'That's why Jesus had no shoes on the crucifix.'

Every cuss! He-Got-It. Babatunde.

He was bare strong though. No one believed he was in Year 10.
He was probably in Year 10 about ten years ago. Hench,
muscles on top of muscles. And he had these long arms that
dropped below he's knees – borderline orang-utan.

I swear, we 'attempted' to rush him one time after school – at
the bus stop. Jerome went to fling him by his rucksack. Blood.
He just, blood, Babatunde just turn't around and did one
fucking… I dunno, it looked sick, he just flung his arm and
Jerome went flying into the bus lane – I thought it was gonna be
some *Final Destination* moment cos the bus proper almost hit
him. Driver slammed the brakes.

Proper close.

Babatunde was blatantly the strongest in our year AND in Year 11 but because he was fresh, he didn't care, he just wanted to get an education. Thing is about my school, certain playboys won't let you get an education without you passing your foundation in street wisdom. Ya gotz ta be streetwise.

Anyway, it was that day in the summertime when all the flying ants start being everywhere. It was interrupting the football and like I said Babatunde TOE-PUNTS the ball over the fence with his size fourteen Oxfam trainer. But what happened next shocked everyone...

(*Pause*.)

He said... (*Shakes his head*.) couldn't believe this.

He said he wasn't getting it!

EVERYONE KNOWS THAT WHOEVER KICKS THE BALL OVER THE FENCE HAS TO CLIMB OVER AND GET IT – simple playground regulations.

He says he ain't getting it – not just that, but the school bell rings, which puts the ball in the position of possibly never being retrieved again! Obviously some passer-by will see that ball, take that ball and make that ball their ball. And it was a good ball too.

Babatunde puts on his blazer and heads out of the playground. Everyone's like –

'Oooh... Liberties!!'

He was taking the PI double. And Terence Cunningham, who the football belonged to, he'd be the last one to go fetch the ball, he got his pride, a reputation to sustain. Terence Cunningham is one of the younger Cali Road Boys, CRB – (*Does the gang hand-sign, fingers forming the letters C, R and B*.) He's older brother, Pierre Cunningham, used to go our school and he was hard as nails. They still whisper his name in the corridors.

'BABATUNDE!!' Terence said.

Baba stopped and turned to face his enemy. Terence Cunningham opens his arms out wide, like wings – (*Demonstrates*.) Animals normally do that as a trick to appear bigger in order to ward off their opponent –

'Is that how it's gonna be?' said Terence.

Then Babatunde just took off his blazer, flung it on the floor hard! The earth shook –

'DO YOU WANT TO FIGHT ME TOO?! EVERY DAY NA THE SAME, SOMEBODY NEW IS WANTING TO FIGHT BABA. MAKE HE NO FIGHT ME-OH! If you fight me your face go be roforofo face, your body go be roforofo body! I done tell him before, make 'e no fight'e'o!'

(*Pause*.)

If I'm totally honest, I think… I might've shitted my pants a little bit when he said that. He was some Nigerian gangster! He laid it on the line! His voice echoed through the playground like a lion's roar through the plains of the Serengeti. *Blood clot*. He had that fire that you only see in the eyes of grown men.

We all looked over to Terence Cunningham. Terence?

Now, there's only ONE THING Terence Cunningham can say that could top *Baba*-tunde's display of sheer *Baba*-rity. And it comes in the form of two words. Nope, It's not 'fuck you' or 'fuck off!' or 'ya mum'. Nah.

It is another set of words that outside of a school means almost nothing.

Terence stood there. Just nodding his head – his face bearing no emotion. Then the two words we were all pregnant to hear rolled off of his tongue and out of his mouth and into our ears –

'3:30.'

Everyone heard that?!?!!

'3:30, blooOOOOood! FIGHT FIGHT FIGHT FIGHT FIGHT FIGHT!'

We went ballistic! I took off my school tie, wrapped it around my fist like a boxing glove and started punching the air. (*Demonstrates*.)

'Fight Fight Fight Fight Fight.'

(*Extremely excited*.) Free-Fur-E.

3:30.

That was IT! Are you mad? Are you unwell? Are you under anaesthesia, fam? We were hyped up, man! We had only fifth and sixth period left – so without further ado, we do what we do best: add fuel to the fire –

'Who'd you think is gonna win?'

'I heard Terence's dad bought him that football for a hundred and seventy-five pound!'

'I bet you Terence's brother comes down!'

'Who, Pierre Cunningham??'

'Baba's gonna get strawberry jam dripping out of his nose.'

'I bet you this – I bet you that.'

'Where's it gonna be?'

Dumb question – errr. About *'where's it gonna be'* – blatantly it's gonna be in the underpass. That's where all the school fights happen...

Kehinde

The day my brother brought this white girl back it was as if Grandma just knew, like she had some sixth sense or something. As soon as she come through the door, she puts the shopping bags down on the kitchen table, where I was watching TV. Normally she'd start packing the food into the fridge, I'd automatically stand up to boil the water for the vegetables before she had a chance to tell me how lazy I was, but no, not today. She marched straight up the stairs and made a beeline to my brother's room – didn't even take off her jacket. Most days, she'd just stand in his doorway and ask him why he weren't doing his homework or why he only vacuumed downstairs but today she must've smelt the sex-funk or something. She went all the way into his room. Shut the door behind her. When I heard that door click shut I had to crack a smile though, cos my brother was always getting away with things. I went and sat on the stairs, didn't wanna miss a sniffle.

White girl is hiding, behind the curtains. Grandma notices the pair of UGG boots sticking out from the bottom. My brother is sat at his desk, with his eyes on a page apparently halfway through some novel. Fooling nobody – he doesn't read. Grandma walks straight over to the curtain and punches it. The curtain screams. She punches it a bag of times. A barrage of punches later and the drapes fall down. She spat in the face of a little white girl somewhere between fourteen and sixteen years old and then gave her the beating of her life.

When she was done she sat on the corner of my brother's bed – sweating, breathing heavily. She had folds of pink skin under her fingernail from when she'd scratched the girl's eyelids. She beat that white girl bad. She beat that white girl like she was the white woman who my granddad cheated on her with. She beat that white girl like she was the white bus driver who closed the doors in her face after she ran all that way to catch it. She beat that white girl like she was the white man in the market who gave her ten pounds' change when she remembers giving him the twenty-pound note that she *just* got from the bank. She beat that white girl the way she would've loved to beat the white woman in customs who made her throw away all the food she had in her hand luggage.

Grandma had a heart condition, so when the white police came to arrest her, the white paramedics came too. She felt that white people had taken everything away from her. So as they were putting her in handcuffs and she was calling them devils and Lucifers and demons, obviously they thought she was crazy. But I knew she wasn't crazy. She wasn't crazy she was just hurt. And conditioned. And that's how she'd be until the perishing day because it's hard trying to tell old people new things when they're stuck in 1974.

My uncle came over to our house that evening and you know what he said to me? He said –

'Kehinde, you are her trophy child, you know that? She has looked after you since you had no teeth so you have to look after her until her teeth fall out.'

Family are so shifty. They are always trying to pass on the responsibility.

Joanne

So we lived in the last house on my road. The only house without a blue door. Mum wouldn't let the council paint it, even though it was free. She believed the Government were fitting cameras in the peepholes.

When I think of that house yeah, all I can think of is 'brown-ness' because everything was so dry 'n' dusty 'n' old 'n' boring 'n' grey 'n'.

It smelt like mold 'n' medicine 'n' vomit 'n' musty bed sheets 'n'.

The curtains were slow death 'n' Mum kept them closed in the daytime, even. Quite depressing.

That's why me and my magnets were in no hurry returning from school.

Blue door, blue door, blue door, black door.

One time, I open the black door and mum was sitting there. Just sitting there, on the stairs. Right on the middle step. Staring into space. (*Looking behind her.*)

'Muuum?' (*Waves her hand in Mum's face.*)

She had soil in her hands. All up in her fingernails. Up to her wrist. Like she had been digging hard. Or gardening with no gloves. She didn't even acknowledge me – real talk. I follow the soiled carpet. I remember standing over the random hole in my garden, looking in it. Nothing. Just wondering why I couldn't speak with my mum, I started praying?

Rugrat

(*Talking over the same words at the end of* JOANNE*'s speech.*)
I started praying.

Praying that some fool wouldn't blab his mouth to a teacher about the fight. See, most teachers in this school are pussies in real life who probably got bullied when *they* were in school, so when they get an opportunity like this, to stop a school fight, they leap at it, makes 'em feel bigger. It gives 'em 'staffroom bragging rights'. Then this teacher would take that velocity, go off to their lesson and bully some Year 10 who has difficulty understanding algebraic expressions. Or threaten me with detention or something – when I *am* trying. I am.

Terence Cunningham yeah, he is hands down the fastest in the school. One hundred metres, two hundred metres, run for da bus, race you to the next lamp post, anything, bruv – no one beats him. He'll even give you a head start. There was no shame in losing a race to him cos he is a speed demon. When he runs, he kicks out his leg and produces these huge strides that cover land, but all that was wasted on the pitch, he's just a goal-hanger.

He got in this fight with a Year 11 when we were in Year 9! BLOOOOOD – sickest fight. One of the sickest fights. All I'm saying is, you know when someone gets fly-kicked in their back and their head proper swings backwards. I remember that in slow motion. Terence Cunningham can definitely fight.

I wanted Barbaric-tunde to batter him though. Terence was out of order sometimes, man, him and the rest of the CRB Youngers. Take that same day yeah, he asked for a DROP of my Fanta Fruit Twist, a drop. I gives him the bottle now – firstly, he proper wraps his fish-lips around it (and I ain't drinking it after that, I might as well kiss him on the lips directly, ya get me, it's the same ting). Secondly, he boxed it back, all of my drink! In one go, like it was a drinking contest, then tries to hand me the bottle back, talking about –

'Dash that in the bin for me.'

(*Kisses his teeth.*)

And then he burped in my face – for no reason. I wanted Babatunde to do that arm thing to him –

'Guys, can you quiet down!'

It's sixth period now. Pure jokes, it's only RE, Mr Taruvangadum. He's my form tutor as well so I'm on a hype ting.

'But, sir, look at your head.'

'Jamie, I'm gonna kick you out!'

'Yeah I know but look at your urgent head though.'

'Get your gear and get out!!'

'But your head is oblong though, sir, I'm just saying it's long, innit, what, I can't say your head is long?'

'OUT!!!'

'Geez, forget this class anyway.'

I walked down the hallway looking in the windows of all the other classrooms. Everyone's got their heads down – pens squiggling.

Ya know it feels so good at the time, getting kicked out, but when you're in the hallway on your Jacks-Jones, you feel lonely like.

I go down the spiral stairs, walking sideways with my back to the wall in case a teacher looks down from the top and sees me.

I go in the toilets and put my hand behind the radiator. I found a Nokia-3210 in there once, so now I always check.

I cruise the school like a ghost. Permanent-ink marker in my hand. I write my nickname:

(*Writing.*) Rugrat. Rugrat. Rugrat.

This. School. Is… Shit.

If. You. Are. Looking. At. This.

You. Are… Officially…

Gay. Married.

Yours. Truly…

Rugrat.

Then I hear a whisper –

'Rugrat.'

'Ah?'

'Your mum.'

'Who's dat, you tramp?'

'I'm your mum, blood.'

'Jerome, you bitch.'

'Ah how'd you know it was me?'

Jerome sticks his head over the top of the cubicle. Anything to show off that he's one of the few boys in my year who have grown a moustache.

'Cos I smelt your breath.'

I check my phone, 3:20.

'Oi, melon head, it's 3:20. So we gotta kill… (*Does the maths on his fingers.*) ten minutes.'

Wanted to go back to RE with Jerome to show Mr Taruvangadum that by throwing me out he only put me with my bredrin –

'Yo. Jerome. What you doing in there anyway?'

'Ah?'

'You floating your logs? Ah? You dropping the kids off at the pool? Oi?'

I prop myself up to look into his cubicle but just before my eyes can focus he puts his hand in my face and pushes my head out. I fell back onto my bum and my permanent marker slid under the sink.

Jerome fiddles around for a bit in the cubicle then swings open the door with his bag slung on one shoulder. Smiles.

'Who's gonna win?'

We walk.

Jerome blatantly wanted Terence Cunningham to win, they were both CRB Youngers, innit.

We walk out the school gates.

Walk down the hill.

We go shop.

I bought a Fanta Fruit Twist – I drank it before Jerome could ask me for some.

We get to the entrance of the underpass and wait.

Before I look at my watch I almost pee myself with adrenalin, in my mind I estimate 3:32. They're probably piling down the stairs by now, pouring out the school gates.

I look at my watch.

'3:20??? I swear we've been waiting for ages.'

'I know.'

Time moves extra-slow when you're waiting for a fight.

3:22. The bus 271 goes by. I look up and you would die if I tell you who was cosy on the upper deck of this bus.

'Oi, Jerome… bruv, is that Babatunde?'

'Babatunde, where you going?'

Jerome grabbed a pebble, small like a raisin and colourful – he dashes it. It bounces off the back window.

When the mob rolled out of those gates it got E-motional. Some next uproar. Me and Jerome held court at the bus stop – had to clap my phone against the red bench for order in the court.

'Ooorder!'

I took the stand and gave testimony about how straight Babatunde's neck was – pretending he didn't see us, begging his own eyes not to wander. By show of hand it was voted that Babatunde deserved to catch a beat-down tomorrow at lunchtime for committing playground statutory offense 22: false almshouse promotion. But before we all boarded our separate buses, Jerome was dying to show us something. He casually unzipped the front bit of his rucksack and held it open for us to see. I looked in the bag. The thing stood upright. I was at the back of everyone but I saw the thing shimmer as it reflected the sun.

Jerome, man.

I think most of us were all suddenly quite glad Baba had caught that bus.

Come the next day we cussed him but we didn't even feel to rush him any more. To be real, I was quite pleased to see him.

TWO

Kehinde

I remember. I spent the whole first day of secondary school
trying to find my twin sister, Taiwo. They put us in different
form groups and different classes. Looked for her
everywhere. Even when I got home she wasn't there. Strolls
through the door an hour and a half later without her school
tie. And she had the phattest grin on her face. She didn't miss
me a little bit. She loved it that we got split up. I hated it. See
that's when I got the light-skin girlfriend; Rachel. But Rachel
wasn't half as smart as Taiwo. And she couldn't draw a circle
like Taiwo. My sister could draw a perfect freehand circle
like no one in this universe. She'd draw circles in my palm
with her finger and I'd close my eyes because it felt nice. She
was just good at everything. And she could hold her breath
underwater for the longest – longer than anybody I know.
Rachel, on the other hand, she couldn't even swim. She
wasn't even pretty but she was mixed-raced so people were
like –

*'Ah saw Kehinde wit dis MIXED-RACED TING, she's buff,
man.'*

She weren't even buff. She weren't that pretty. Not like Taiwo,
my sister is pretty. You can tell straight away she's pretty. She
has small eyes and big lips and small teeth. And she has this big
mole in her eyebrow.

I couldn't speak to Rachel about anything really. When I got
fed up of kissing and fingering her I'd just start thinking about
Taiwo, start wondering what she was up to. If it was after
school then she was probably playing football. Rachel's dad
worked for the council and he supported the school team so
even he knows how good my sister is playing midfield.
Rachel's dad genuinely liked me –

'You're a golden opportunity, Kehindy,' he'd say.

He was nice, even though he pronounce my name as Kehindy. Kehinde. But he was the first white man that I felt comfortable around, so I didn't correct him.

Rugrat

Four mornings out of five I'm late for school, guaranteed. I mean, they're lucky I even showed up to that ramshackle of a school anyway. When I'm really late, I see a whole group of different faces on the bus. Like this one girl, Jodie. She is so ridiculously buff? It's ridiculous. Gimme heartburn, that girl. She rocks the burgundy uniform cos she goes to EGA Sixth Form. That stands for Elizabeth Garrett Anderson but for us EGA stands for Every Girl Available. No one believes me but I kissed her one time, Jodie.

Swear down – on my mum's life. Before I even started secondary school.

'Twas the summer holiday before Year 7. Who do I see riding her bike through my area? Jodie, the queen of buffness. Courage from within took surface and I told her to stop and then I told her I wanna kiss her round the corner, so she walked her bike round the corner, where I was waiting patiently.

When we kissed her name was Joanne – and she was bless. But school made her remix it to Jodie; her evil side. *Joanne* was nice though. I had my hands on her cold thighs and everything.

When my washing machine broke down I got to see her at the launderette. She used to gel her hair down to her forehead – and it would come down to the side like this – (*Demonstrates.*) Fuck me though, was Jodie rude? That girl was roo-oode! Rude! No one could tell her nothing, boi. She didn't even have to touch you, she'll just drop you one line that'll feel like a t'ump in da face.

One time she roasted this woman on the bus for no reason. No reason! In front of everyone. The woman, all the woman did was ask Jodie politely, to put out her cigarette –

'Who the fuck are you with your penguin shoes, don't chat to me with your breath smelling like wet ass-crack…rah rah rah.'

Motormouth Jodie.

I was pissed when she started going out with Baker. Baker ya know. She had her pick of anyone in the world and she chooses him? He was the dumbest guy in our year. No one will ever truly know how dumb this guy was unless they was in our year. He came out with stupid shit, every single day – of his life. He had dumbness on tap. After a while it just stopped being funny cos, I mean, how can someone be so consistently dumb? Jodie went with him of all people, virginity and everything. Bareback – no protection. Watch Baker come into school the next day walking sideways, talking about his leg is hurting –

'She banged me, bruv, she banged me.'

I was P I doubled. I would've banged her properly. Cos thing is, if you know Baker you know he would've just lied there.

Bitch.

Still love her though.

Joanne

Kristina was this Lithuanian girl who I worked with at the launderette. She had really really bad teeth. What made it worst, she was young. Her breath never used to smell or nothing, her teeth were just bad that's all. She was really pretty when she smiled like this – (*Demonstrates a closed-mouth smile.*)

The launderette was a flippin' electrical mess. Why was the ceiling leaking tumble-dryer water onto the wires for the washing machines? One dirty hazard cycle.

DeathTrap.com, forwardslash, OneDaySomeCustomerGonna-
CatchTheirElectrocutionUpInThisBitchAndSueForAMillion-
Pound – Straight – Real Talk. Nuff people got electric shock
from just leaning on the dryer, ya know. Or from opening the
machine door.

One time, this woman put her carpet in the washing machine. It
washed it yeah, but when it was time for it to come out it wasn't
having it. It was stuck. The water must've made it inflate or
something because initially it was kinda easy to put it in but
pulling it out was the longest.

Me and Kristina tried everything, we were sweating. Was kinda
fun though. When things like that happen at work it's exciting.

The lady whose carpet it was stood out in the street waving down
random guys to come and help us. Like, three different men came
and tried but it wouldn't budge. Then this boy come. He was
kinda skinny compared to the men who had tried and failed. He
had his headphones in and everything, like it was gonna be a
breeze. Anyway he tries for like half a minute then says –

'I'll be back.'

Me and Kristina kinda giggled cos now he's looking kinda cute
in his bright white vest with his skinny self looking all
undernourished. Real talk. And when he said –

'I'll be back.'

his voice was staggeringly deep and freaky like –

'I'll be back.'

(*Giggles, flirting.*) *'Okay, we ain't going nowhere.'*

He left his iPod and his T-shirt on the bench.

The radio behind the till was one of them radios that stay fuzzy,
always stuck in between stations, so I thought I'd listen to his
iPod instead. The tunes were all right still. Skinny boy's got a
little taste.

He comes back. Erm. Why did he bring with him about ten boys
from the estate? They all rode up on their bikes – Myles, Cain,
Obi, Jacob… even my half-brother come but he doesn't speak

to me anyway so… Reuben, Kwame, Rommell, Andrew, Harry, Omar, Hassan, Ibrahim – all of the older lot. Left their bikes spread out on the pavement, making it hard for people to walk past. It wasn't a big launderette but they all squeezed in to try this carpet –

'I bet you any money I'm the one that gets it out, fam.'

They made it a competition. It caused one massive scene, people from other shops were trying to peek in to see what the big crowd was about.

One by one, they tried, pulling at this carpet from different angles. It was like Excaliburs, sword in the stone.

When they got tired of that, they started chatting up Kristina, dropping game on her –

'How comes I ain't never beheld your buffness round here before?'

But when they saw the brown bits on her teeth they all backed off and started cussing each other for chatting to her –

'You're the one that spoke to her, blood, you wanna lips her teeth.'

I felt for her a bit, man – real talk, cos sometimes customers would be like talking about her teeth, blatant, in the shop like she wasn't there. Anyway, all the boys from the estate clear out and ride off on their bikes. Skinny-iPod boy, stays.

Kehinde

I'm in Year 9 at school.

There was this group of boys. The Cali Road Boys. 'CRB' – (*Demonstrates using the hand signs.*) All of them were white, but they made exceptions for *certain* black boys. Like, if you truly supported Arsenal you were allowed in or… if your dad did all kinds of madness that the white boys' dads knew about – things like that. I got sent out of class once but that weren't enough to qualify for the CRB, they only recruited bad breeds. Boys who never bring a pen into school.

A few of them played in the football team. The leader of the CRB was our team striker, his name was Pierre Cunningham. Pierre Cunningham reckoned he could run faster than my sister, and one day during PE he actually said it out loud. Everyone laughed at him of course. Taiwo was *fffast,* the fastest in our year. And she had a really quick start, *zing,* that's how she'd stay ahead the whole race. When she's racing, she should wear a T-shirt with the number '2' on the back so that whoever is behind her knows where they're coming. Second. She is always ahead of whoever is coming second.

After school, the race, was on.

It was, whoever makes it to the fourth lamp pole first, wins.

'On your marks get set GOOO!'

Pierre went early, he had a false start. Everyone saw he ran before we said 'go', he was ahead, but that was cool, no worries, Taiwo was catching up quick. She ran with her back straight, by this time Pierre had already started to swing his shoulders, his form was all messy; means he's tired. When he runs he kicks his foot out so he gets these big strides – an advantage but not a threat. Taiwo had smaller strides but she has good technique, her back, straight – you could iron your clothes on it. Her arms, cutting through the air, *zing-zing-zing,* her feet, moving so swift they barely touched the ground, *zing-zing-zing.* They're neck and neck. They whizz past the launderette at the same time. Pierre's steps were getting heavier and heavier, he was running his hardest, his cheeks were wobbling, but look at Taiwo, the image of composure. Then after they passed the third lamp pole, *ZING-ZING-ZING – Wow.* My sister was holding back all that time. She was only toying with him, she had a LOT left in the reserve… the way she crucified that last twenty metres, boy. Should've seen Pierre Cunningham's face drop. She ran so fast that her shadow had to catch up. He crossed the lamp post a couple seconds later and put his hands on his knees Straight Away.

Taiwo was already at the fifth lamp post, the momentum, cos she was going so fast, the momentum carried her to flipping…

the next hemisphere; she had to walk back. Victory walk.
(*Watching her walking back.*) Just cool, not out of breath or
nothing, didn't even break a sweat, didn't even complain about
Pierre's false start or about the random bikes blocking the
pavement, just smiling, grinning them small teeth. Then her
smile turned into furrowed eyebrows.

(*A boy in crowd.*) '*Yeah! What did I tell you? I knew Pierre was
gonna win! He's t-too fast, no no no, he's th-th-three fast, no no
no, he's f-f-f-four fast!*'

Some people were saying that Pierre won!

Joanne

Cute-skinny-iPod-boy gives it one last try. He takes his boney
arm that looks like the letter 'L', sticks it in the machine, feels
about a bit, turns to carpet lady –

'*Did you fold it before you put it in?*'

He asks –

'*One of the corners are trapped.*'

He puts his arm in deeper, and *pop*, the corner come out.

Facile.

Then with two fingers he pulls the whole carpet out. So easily. It
was like magic.

Carpet lady was grateful, she started dancing and all sorts, like
it was some nuff expensive carpet. Calling him Aladdin, saying
that the magic carpet wouldn't move for anyone but Aladdin. I
was laughing cos now he kinda looks like Aladdin. Aladdin's
skinny, innit.

Don't think carpet lady didn't slip and fall on her backside
when she was dancing around! I was cracking up – Real Talk.
Cos true she was kinda big, carpet lady. Skinny boy was trying

to avoid my eye contact because he would've started cracking too. He helped her to her feet now, but erm… why was her breast blatantly hanging out her bra?

I was like –

'Oi, carpet lady, you're indecent, innit. Your titty, is swinging.'

(*Gestures to pull up bra.*)

Boy. I dunno.

I offered to dry her carpet for free.

She said she didn't wanna risk it.

I do not blame her. Could be another episode.

Hear this, she wouldn't let cute skinny boy leave until he let her reward him with an ice cream from the off-licence next door. Hilarious. Like he was some little boy. That killed me.

He came over and mouthed something to me but I had his headphones in. I handed him back his iPod just as I finished listening to this exclusive Slum Village song that I hadn't heard before, the chorus ended up stuck in my head for days afterwards.

(*She sings a few lines from the chorus of 'Climax (Girl Shit)' by Slum Village.*)

He offered me his ice cream. So sweet –

'Sorry but I don't like Solero.'

The next week he comes into the launderette with a white-chocolate Magnum ice cream. My favourite. And I didn't even tell him, ya know. Obviously I had to give him my number immediately, no long ting. Sorry but, from time a brudda can just KNOW your favourite ice cream, you gotta take that brudda serious – real talk. And not a day goes by after that that I don't think of him. He said his name was Baker. What kinda name is Baker? I just call him Aladdin.

(*Singing.*) *'Like a dream come true…'*

Kehinde

Pierre?! Nah! Pierre didn't win shit!

They were only saying that because they were afraid of him and the Cali Road Boys. Look at Pierre's face, he knows he lost. He weren't showing off like he does when he gets it in the back of the net. Yo Pierre!! (*Walking up to him.*)

He's taller than me but I made sure I got in his face –

'Why deceive yourself, fam? Why, fam? You lost. Accept it. Digest it. Look, look at this, this is the letter 'L', you should eat it. You should marry it. You earned it. You can't win all the time. CRB? Who… Why would anyone wanna be in your scabby crew? I lost mad respect for you, fam. Epic Fail'

Instead, what really came out was –

'Ah Pierre, gotta give it to you, bro, you're kinda fast, that was close but you won, by an inch though, just an inch, that was close but you won, you had a better start, she should've dipped.'

SHIIIT!

What's wrong with me?

My eyes dart over his shoulder in search of Taiwo. Phew. She was occupied, she didn't clock.

That's when I heard a crow caw from the tree above and… there was *something* about this moment.

You… you know when you're brushing your teeth in the morning and you suddenly remember you had a dream last night and you just kinda freeze up in front of the mirror because you're trying to recall it and you almost had it just now but it slipped away? And you have to let it go, carry on brushing and try to forget about it because you know that the more you try and remember it, the further it's gonna repress itself deep down into your inner psyche? *That* feeling. When I heard the crow caw in the tree it jugged something in the quicksand part of my mind and gave me *that* feeling. I knew there was some kinda lesson to be learnt, I felt as though I were reliving a parable.

A CRB throws his scabby arm over my shoulder.

'Who's the fastest in the year, bruv?'

'Err it used to be Taiwo but now it's Pierre,' I said quickly.

Then the pin dropped. I realised what the muffled fluttering under my subconscious was about. It swung my rationale into the story Mr Taruvangadum taught us earlier that day.

Right before they captured Jesus, when he was chilling with his Apostles, he said to Simon Peter –

'Before the cock crow twice, thou shalt deny me thrice.'

It was obvious. The crow's caw was the cock's first crow. Sounds crazy I know but it was a sign.

Up in the tree, the crow stared directly down at me. I barely understood the omen, when Pierre grabbed me by the strap of my school bag and lead me to the middle –

'... even Kehindickle saw!! Tell 'em what you saw, go on, tell 'em.'

I looked up at the crow. My sister's face shot out to me from the crowd.

'Errr. You... Pierre won. Taiwo should've dipped.'

The crow cawed a harsh final cry then flew from the tree. Taiwo heard. She turns her head in shame.

Shit.

That rendered me horrendous.

I pulled my tongue out of Pierre's bumhole and let it back in my mouth where it should've stayed.

FUCK!

I tried to explain to her that –

'I swear down, he won by an inch, I'm telling you, from where I was standing, at the angle from which I saw it, he won by an inch – plus, the sun was in my eye, you should've dipped.'

– to obvious no avail. She had no words for me, she wouldn't even look in my face.

'Oi...'

She zipped open her rucksack, barely listening to my false apologia, turned and articulated one thing:

'You have SO much to learn.'

That shot me through my bad heart ten times –

Ruptured my spleen,
fractured my ribs,
internal bleeding,
haemorrhages,
blood clot,
cataracts,
brain damage,
heart attack.

Death by double-crossing. My one person in the world. If I were allowed to have one person in the world, I'd have Taiwo.

As I watch her put her trainers into the carrier bag before she puts them in her rucksack, I promised myself I would never shun a *blessing* to gain friends ever again. Right then and there, I grew up. Inside here – (*Touches his heart.*) And the growing pains sent a tear rolling down my cheek. I had to pull myself together, quickly.

Taiwo slung her bag over her shoulder and we began our trek home.

The loser had to kiss the winner's shoe, so Pierre and his pack kept howling offences. They even started following us home, said they'd leave when she kissed his shoe. Taiwo won that race, fair and square, she was not about to get on her knees to kiss a loser's shoelaces. She told Pierre that to his face. They got all sore. They started throwing stones. We just kept walking, trying to ignore them.

Looking back in hindsight, I should've seized that moment to redeem myself, but I shoulda woulda coulda – at the time I was too cut up inside. Not a blood cell or one scintilla in me was invested in heroics. I kept my head down like a professional coward and I tightened my punani.

'Pussy!'

The stones were flying past us. Some of them were rebounding off of car windows, some of them were small like little tablets – hitting my school bag. One of the mixed-raced CRB had a whole handful of pebbles, ran up to Taiwo and put it down the back of her school shirt. She let him do it. Helped him even by slowing down a little so he could pull his wrist out of her shirt collar more comfortably. They all cheer as if it were some wonderful magic trick what he did. The stones dribbled down the bottom of her untucked shirt and beat the ground with every step she took. Occasionally I'd get one in the back of the head but it didn't hurt that much because I was *blessed* with hair that curls over itself, softening the blow, therefore protecting me from things like sharp stones that otherwise would cut me deep. Besides, they were aiming for my sister.

This had gone on for some time now and I could tell she was getting tired of being strong. She stopped and turned around to say something wise probably. That's how they got her in the face. As soon as it left Pierre's fingers he regretted it. He watched it cut through the air, this one was flying on course. The way he dashed it, sideways like he wanted it to skid-bounce across the lake surface. That one was small like a raisin and colourful like racism. It just missed her eye by about a centimetre, embedding itself underneath her skin. But then on this occasion, contrary to the song, the *second* cut was the deepest. Another CRB pitcher lent in with a right arm. This one pitched like he was a descendant of Babe Ruth. It clipped the side of her head. Sending blood trickling around the shape of her ear, down her neck, onto her school shirt and making CRB scatter like P – I – G – E – O – N – S.

Fled. All but one. Pierre, transfixed with eyes a-glaze. He was sorry. There are many ways you can put the fear of God in a child but when they do bad on their own volition and become stained with guilt from it, well... suffice to say a lesson is learnt.

'Yes, bruv, she bleeds. Just like you.'

I felt like her younger brother sometimes. Taiwo was a lot wiser than me, but by culture, even though I came out second, I'm the older twin.

In my tribe, we name the first-born of twins Taiwo. Which means:

'The first to taste the world.'

The second-born is normally called Kehinde, that's my name, it means:

'The last to come.'

But the reason it's said that I'm older, even though my sister was the first-born, is because Kehinde is the one that *sends* Taiwo out of the womb. Kehinde asks Taiwo to check what the world is like outside and to report back. Taiwo is subsequently born. She then communicates to Kehinde spiritually, through the sound of her cries, she lets him know whether life is going to be one of suffering and running or one that's virtuous and playful. Taiwo's reply determines if Kehinde will be born alive or stillborn. So despite me being born second, I'm still the true elder of the twins because I sent Taiwo on an errand. A prerogative of one's elders in Yoruba-land.

Doctors had to shave her head to sew the stitches – same like they do furry pets. She had the whole school in hysterics the day she came back because she had an eyepatch on one side and a shaved head on the other. Only thing she was missing was a hook for a hand and a parrot for her shoulder. Even Mr Taruvangadum laughed at her and he's the RE teacher!

But she was so cool with that, she let everyone laugh it up, she laughed *with* them. She was sooo cool. And in the playground she still played football, except this time, instead of having some indignant defender in goal, she volunteered to be the goalkeeper.

That match was heavy, I joined in, the sun was out, my heart was pounding properly and I didn't get out of breath, not once. When she headered me the ball, I knew she'd forgiven me. She forgave me like Jesus forgave Simon Peter. I watched her in goal. Her smile was back on. Full beam.

Then Pierre and his crew came, like the cloud that blocks the sun. Pierre grabbed the ball and blasted it over the fence. On purpose. Another bid to get a reaction out of Taiwo. All because he got beat by the black girl – who he was deeply in love with. He should've just forgot about what his boys would think and told her that he loved her.

Joanne

When my mum got sectioned I was given some leaflet about a foster retreat. Leaflet had bright colours on the front and all the children in the picture were happy, smiling, daisy-picking, unisex-shirt-and-dungarees-wearing, bright-eyed, *'I went swimming in the LAKE this morning'* type-of-lifestyle-having-looking children. It was up north somewhere. I was getting kinda sick of London, school, people, nosey neighbours, oh my God, NOSEY! Who haven't got the slightest. Who just assume and make up stories and who don't actually know the real FACTS about my mum, and who may find themselves very knocked out, dazed and amazed, if they chat to me sideways, again – real talk.

I was just very bored of all that shi-*T*. Wanted a change of pace. And I felt like I'd stuck my magnet to everything ferromagnetic. I wanted to experience something different so when I got that leaflet I thought, bless, why not? I'll chill with these perfect-life-having children for a summer up north, might do me some good. Maybe like –

Actually wait… I have to go back and finish my story about the launderette because it got a bit mad. My bad…

Remember the carpet fing? One of the first men who tried to help with the carpet was some Greek-looking guy, thick glasses

– funny accent – grey hair – stomach big, like a pregnant woman, nine months. He was lingering a lot afterwards, around the launderette. Few weeks go by and why do me and Kristina notice he's been following us home every weekend? Nasty. But what was even more fucked up: when he came into the launderette, he'd try chat to me. He'd show up, briefcase in hand and it was like he was speaking in verse, being all lyrical and stuff, saying he wanted to *taste* me, talking so slick you could see the crude oil on his tongue. It was blatantly something that he'd rehearsed in the mirror. I'd just tell him straight no chaser –

'Listen, old man, I'm not in the mood for romancing with some weirdo, ya get me, so don't waste your rotten breath, innit, you'll need it to blow out your hundred and fifty candles at your birthday next year, that's if you're lucky to make it through the night with your slow heartbeat like some kinda reptile, and your deep eye sockets, looking like a skeleton already, walking in here dressed like Inspector Morse with your empty briefcase – just trying to look smart, wearing the same suit that they'll bury you in at your funeral. LISTEN! Next time you roll up in here you better have some garments to wash or I will leave you in a grisly state…'

(*A long kiss of the teeth.*)

You can't leave *any* hope for them people, ya know. About you want to *taste* me, *are you drunk on battery acid? Don't make me vomit, sir.*

Looking at me with his Lucifer eyes.

Had to tell him straight, but Kristina though, Kristina would really chat to him, like really chat to him. Anyway, cut a long story short she started feeling the old boy. A little too much. Did everything he said. Launderette was a sweat box but he made her cover up her arms. Then he made her wear a longer skirt to cover up her legs. And before I left, it was obvious that he started beating her because she was covering up her bruises too. With make-up – real talk. Makes me think, is that what good girls get for having bad teeth?

On my last day at the launderette I got the phattest electric shock from the washing machine. I think it was saying goodbye.

THREE

Joanne

I dunno… the retreat was… alright. But everyone was younger than me, which was kinda disappointing – having no one your age there to chat to.

It looked NOTHING like the flyer. Them dere people who made the flyer are jokers – real talk. I gets there now, all the colours had faded on the building. The children there were looking crustified, dear Lord; crust! I thought I had it bad. One of them looked like she was wearing a potato sack. Another one look like he stole his clothes off of a scarecrow. Caveman couture as well; no shoes. Some people do not have it. It's a sad world, man.

On the first day you could tell who and who were gonna clash. It was like the Big Brother House for Teenage Rejects and Unwanted Infants. Some dramatic kids up in there, boy. Crying like it was first day of school. Little Jack was crying like he sold his cow for some beans and never got the beanstalk – real talk. I told everyone straight –

'Oi oi, listen! I'm the oldest here, innit. So like… yeah… just… just have respect and dat… For me.'

Ah, I flopped it, innit. Like George Bush, I had everyone's attention and flopped severely. You know when you tell everyone to stop, and then everyone actually stops dead like, and they're all just looking at you, and that kinda surprises you because you never thought they would pay you any mind, so you forget what you was gonna say? Real Talk.

(*Mocking herself.*) *'…just have respect for me and dat.'*

We were *all* fucked up in that place anyhow so I blended in nicely with that intro.

There was this girl, Frankie. I think Frankie's a crack-baby, the most hyperest thirteen-year-old in the world. She already had this raspy voice and she was always screaming and shouting and talking (bitching) and laughing or whistling that loud whistle, the one where you jam up two fingers in your mouth – I hate when people do that indoors. Why? I beg, it's not necessary –

'Okay Frankie, we all know you can do it now, stop showing off – REAL!'

And boy was she oversexed. Always chatting wet 'bout some boy who was banging her doggy-style under some bridge after dark. Then I'll overhear her telling someone else the same story but she'd say it was on *top* of the bridge before sunset. Lying through her muddy braces. A mad house. But I actually started to enjoy myself...

Rugrat

NOW.

There was this special school trip. For RE. We had to go on a pilgrimage. A pilgrimage is when you take a walk towards God. It's meant to bring you closer to the G-man himself. You're meant to go as you are, imperfect. Some people go with their sickness, some wanna give thanks and others are just curious. Us? We were forced to go. Didn't wanna be there to save my dog's life.

Had to walk some long ting. Proper long. Must've been like thirty of us trekking through fields and shit. It had rained as well. And we could proper see the rainbow. We looked up at it – (*He looks.*) clean across the sky. I swear by the time we looked back in front of us everyone was gone.

It was just me, Jerome and Baker. Lost.

At first we were scared but then we thought, *'Fuck it.'* The sun came out and dried everything up quick time. We walked past some green gardens, cows, some old church. You wouldn't think there'd be stray cats out in the countryside, would you? There was. Couldn't believe it. Baker spotted it. He was like –

'Oi, blood, that rabbit looks bizarre.'

(*Sotto*.) He's so dumb.

'If it's a cat, then what's it doing in the bush? Who takes care of it?'

Baker.

Anyway, we kept walking, past farmers and sheep, sheepdogs. Was kinda therapeutic. It was the first time in our lives that we just 'walked'.

Ten minutes went by where nobody said nothing, just marching like.

The sun started rising down. We got to a village. It was dead-out. Ghost town. We saw some old man walking his little rat-dog. Weirdest thing though as well, cos I *know* I saw this one black brudda in the distance. (*Intrigued as he watches him*.) I got good eyesight, innit, and he defo ain't with us on this pilgrimage ting. I went to a joke like – (*Turns to get the attention of his boys*.)

'Yo, Jerome, why's your uncle…'

(*Turning back to the black man*, RUGRAT *is perplexed to find he's no longer there*.)

Just like that. The brudda wasn't there.

Anyway, we arrived at this old bridge. Stopped in front of it. I saw it and was like –

'Fuck me, that's an old bridge.'

Kehinde

By Year 10, me and Rachel were still friends but she weren't my girl. The incident with the CRB brought me and Taiwo closer so I didn't need a girlfriend any more after that. But we were still cool though, Rachel and I. We were both taking a few early GCSE's so we went to the library together – things like that. On one evening after the library we went back to hers. We randomly kissed in the library that day and we were gonna do some more at her house or something. Her dad was home, I heard him creak the floorboard upstairs. He didn't mind me being there ever. He came down the stairs slowly when he heard us that day. Caught us as we were mixing Ribena in the kitchen, he told Rachel to leave, she took my Ribena glass with her to the sitting room so I'd join her afterwards, he sat me down at the dinner table and told me that Taiwo had drowned at the lido and that she was in a better place now. He twisted his keys in his hand as he spoke to me. He would drive me home.

When the car stopped at the traffic lights, I jumped out and ran. Ran until I didn't recognise the streets. Until the parked cars looked more expensive. Until the houses got further apart from each other. Until the people were shades paler in colour. Until nothing could remind me of Taiwo.

I just thought I'd feel it, ya know, her being my twin. We Yoruba believe both twins share one soul. So if one twin dies, the soul is disturbed – leaving the other twin unbalanced.

There's this ritual. The making of the Ere Ebeji. It's meant to balance my soul.

The Ifá Priest chooses the best carver from my village back home, one who knew my ancestors. The carver is asked to make an Ere Ebeji; a small wooden figure of Taiwo.

The head was big in proportion to the body because that's where her spirit is transported to. And although it looks nothing like Taiwo, the figure is to be as respected and as powerful as the person it represents.

Grandma treated it as if it were real. She bathed it, fed it, and in the winter, clothed it. On my birthday, it'd be put out on display. Cos it would be her birthday too. And Grandma put it in my school bag on random days. I'd get to first lesson, unzip my bag and find that wooden piece of shit in there and I'd just wanna smash it.

Forgive me, ancestors, Ifá Priest and all believers of the ritual, for I am bold to say the least that it did not balance my soul.

One day, when the world was enough, when I couldn't bear it, when I couldn't get the image of Pierre's clenched teeth as he held my sister's head under the water out of my mind, I went up north to do something stupid. Something very foolish – to myself. Something that only people who hate their lives do. But there, I met a girl. She saved me. She saved me from myself.

You never know who God is gonna take back next, but at the same time you never know who God is gonna bring into your life. Joanne.

Joanne

I slipped in the shower again. This time I had to have my arm in a sling for a week. So while the others went abseiling and did all them DUMB activities, I stayed back at the retreat. Reading. Writing poems a bit. I had that Slum Village tune on religious repeat.

(*Singing.*) *'Being wid you all alone is like a dream come true'* – I can't sing, innit.

I was mentally illing myself in the mirror one day. Just dissecting my – I fucking hate my chin, I was imagining it smaller when Kehinde bussed in. He apologised like a madman

for not knocking first. Said he didn't know anyone was here,
that I was in his old room –

KEHINDE. So sorry, I used to come here, I'm just helping out
this week.

JOANNE. He was from London as well. Whenever he spoke he
placed his hand on the back of his neck.

KEHINDE. Have you met Mrs Butler? Did she tell you the
story about the boy who never leaves? That's me, innit. I still
can't believe she gave you my room, I thought I was
exclusive.

JOANNE. I swear he KILLED me with the neck thing. You
know when someone does something sweet and then you
love them straight away. Everything they do after that is
voodoo, just hooks you. I died about ten times speaking with
him. I felt like I stumbled across the most humble prince.
He's really a duke or a prince but he doesn't know it yet.

(*To* KEHINDE.) Oi, Kehinde, I'm gonna tell you everything
about my life and you can tell me what you think, okay?

Rugrat

Was one of them arch bridges made of old grey rocks and that.

We jammed at the middle of the bridge, at its highest point
which wasn't that high. It was a small bridge and below on
either side, where there probably once was a running stream,
was now a house with a garden. Both these houses were
derelict. One of the roofs had caved in. Baker starts hanging
his upper body over the bridge, peering into one of the houses.
Me and Jerome are on the opposite side, just taking in the
purple-and-blueberry sky. It's okay. I mean… everything's
okay when skies are that colour, innit. Now I'm thinking about
that brudda again. Dunno why but I'm thinking deep about
him still – I know I didn't imagine it. The way he just
disappeared.

I mean he *was* standing kinda close to the cliff edge – well, I looked away and like. Dunno. Maybe he –

'Oi oi oi, you lot, there's a baby over here,' said Baker.

Thing is right. If it was anyone else, you might – MIGHT! – believe them right? They wouldn't randomly say there was a baby out in the woods, and I'm normally not a doubting Thomas, but because it was Baker…

'I swear down, it's… it's a little baby.'

In my heart, deep down, I knew, there wasn't a baby there, there was no such thing. That's one of the stupidest things Baker's ever come with. So Jerome and I blanked him. That was until, we heard what sounded like a noise from a baby.

'Hello, little baby,' said Baker

Jerome and I crossed over to Baker's side of the bridge and to our surprise when you lean your body over the bridge and you look to your left – and if Jerome got his melon head out of the way! – you could see a baby. A baby. In the sticks. Under a bridge. Somewhere up north. We got lost and found a baby. I couldn't imagine that wild shit. I turn to Baker –

'I can see the little baby now.'

'Told you.'

Joanne

Kehinde didn't have much advice. But he listened well and he was honest.

He said I was crazy. To which I replied, *'True indeed, tell me somethin' that I don't already know, blood.'*

Then he said I should write a novel because I got nuff mad stories and dat. My reply to that was – *'Real Talk.'*

Don't know how practical that would be, a fifteen-year-old manic-depressive, fucking... orphan child, writing a booklet for other people to actually read and dat but – *Real Talk*. Cos he had a point, I do have mad testimonies.

He said that I needed to tell Baker I was having his baby. I replied – *'Fuck Off!'* In a venomous rage. Dunno why. Touchy subject, parenthood. Well... with me anyway. It's touchy.

I seriously felt kinda guilty that all because of me... Kehinde had to sleep in a stuffy little cupboard across the hall. It could barely fit a single bed.

Rugrat

Countryside. Up north. Us lot. Lost. On a pilgrimage that we didn't wanna be on. Under a troll's bridge. We see a baby. I was looking at it.

I'm feeling kinda woozy so I quit hanging off this bridge and get back on my feet. Jerome and Baker are still hanging down the side of this bridge. The head rush clears and I scope my surroundings. Not a *soul* in sight. I'm standing on a bridge and there's a baby underneath. Probably directly underneath me. Jesus Christ –

'Oh! That was close,' said Jerome.

'I got it, bruv, what you talking about?' says Baker.

'No you didn't,' said Jerome.

'I did,' says Baker.

Them lot started seeing who can spit on the baby.

(*Spits.*)

'Oh! It's looking at me.'

'Come here, baby.'

(*Spits.*)

Ah man. I dunno. I dunno, a week ago I'd be down there spitting with them.

'If I was where you are I'd get a bull's eye.'

'Come here, little baby.'

Temperature drop. In both heart and atmosphere. It's getting cold.

'Look, Baker, the baby's got your fish eyes,' said Jerome.

'Shut up… nah wait, Baby does kinda look like me still,' said Baker.

That's when I automatically blurted out –

'Him and Jodie had a son!'

I didn't have to say that. And it burns me that I'm joining in but it naturally just –

'Him him him and Jodie had a bush baby, innit, you been carrying him all this way, Baker?'

(*Quickly covers his mouth with his hand before he can say more.*)

They laughed.

'See look, if that's not my spit on its nose then what?' says Baker.

'Rugrat! Where you at?'

I'm here, man.

I can't watch them. It's not good. They're playing with God. They're spitting on a little helpless baby.

'Please, oi, you lot, come let's go, man.'

They stand up straight.

'Whoa, head rush. Baker, you can't get a head rush, can you?' said Jerome.

'Come we just go, man.'

Baker has this pebble in his hand. He throws it high and catches it –

'I bet you any money that I can dash this on the baby with my eyes closed.'

Joanne

That night, I couldn't sleep. Frankie next door was killing me with the noises, having finger-sex with herself. So I goes up the hall to Kehinde's cupboard-room, quieter there, innit. I stood outside it for about ten minutes. I was stuck. My feet were cemented. I wanted to go in but it had a black door.

Blue door, blue door, blue door, black door.

Kehinde must've felt my presence because he opened up slowly and peeked his head out. Either that or he could see my shadow underneath his door. He assured me I had nothing to worry about and he said that the door was blue underneath, that when he used to come here, the door was blue. He even found a bit on the bottom of the door where the painter had missed a spot. It was baby blue –

KEHINDE. Told you.

JOANNE. He said.

To which I replied –

'Get over it, fam, not like it's the only blue door on planet Earth, fam, it's nothing to congratulate or celebrate, fam, it's not like you've just hit the jackpot, fam – real talk.'

But secretly I was mad relieved that the door was baby blue.

We laid in his small cot. And obviously I've jammed with boys before but Kehinde was on some different echelon. We were communicating on some next wavelength – dolphin frequency. He just starred at me for ages like – right in my eyes like he

could see directly to my soul. Like he tapped a channel to my
spirit. That's him though, he just looks at me and I'm liquidised
– not even on no sexual ting – come like Cyclops Polyphemus
the way he be watching me. Well, it felt like that anyway. That's
when I clocked he was a blue magnet. Him blue and me red.
The way we attracted was as if he already had a magnet
vacancy. As if I was filling up a space that was once inhabited.
See, just when I thought I had conquered the world of
ferromagnetism, behold, Kehinde the blue magnet; cool on the
outside and hot in the middle.

He combed his fingers through my hair. And he discovered the
scar on my head – (*Indicates a scar, it's in the same region as
Taiwo's scar.*)

And I remembered Mum. And he remembered someone. And a
tear rolled down my cheek and onto his chest. And I used my
finger as the pen, and my tears as the ink, to draw perfect circles
on his chest as the canvas. And then a single kiss came down
and landed on my head and it was suspended there for a while.
He held me tight. And he said –

'*Finally.*'

(*Touched.*) '*Finally.*' He said '*Finally.*' About *me*. No one's ever
waited for me before.

I never knew so many emotions could hit you at the same time.
And the thought that there was no guarantee, no promise, that I
would ever meet another soul who would hold me like he did
that night, made my heart beat out of control like his own.
Made my head explode. In that moment, I swear, I was forced
to grow the fuck up. I said to myself –

(*In tears.*) '*Jodie. Nah nah. Joanne. You're not a little girl no
more, y'understand. You gotta use this – (Points to head.) now.
More crucial than ever. No, it hasn't been all roses but move –
the fuck – on. You're a big girl. Fuck…*'

I was crying, boy. I don't cry. I never cry. But I was crying –
real talk.

Then the following morning, Kehinde, 'the boy who never
leaves', had to leave. Abruptly.

Boy.

I don't know what I got that's making them leave. If ever loved by a magnet like Kehinde you have been loved totally. This magnet will pry apart your ribs, ram its hand into your chest cavity, steal all of your heart, and leave the phattest scar 'cross your chest just so's you never forget.

I *could* tell you that him just suddenly leaving didn't take the piss out of my life completely, that it didn't leave me unbalanced, that it didn't relaunch misery.

Rugrat

There's no real reason why Baker wants to stone the baby. No reason.

I look to the end of the bridge and I swear I can see that black brudda.

Just there. He's standing there.

Clocking me. Come like he knew I was thinking of him. But he was behind us though. I ain't got nothing for him.

'Go on then, four pound,' said Jerome.

'Deal,' says Baker.

He's just standing there like.

His shirt is blowing hard in the wind like it was when he was standing near the cliff. But it ain't windy though – what the fuck, man.

Baker throws the stone at the baby.

'OH! That was close, bruv, but you missed, gimme my four pound,' says Jerome.

'Double or nothing.'

'Well, you might as well bring my eight pound right now, fam, deal.'

They shake hands. The atmosphere is ripped. Cold. (*Shivers*.)

But look at this brudda. Can't tell if he's staring me out cos I can't get focus on his eyes, too tough. He's right there but I don't feel if he's there for definite or not. Why am I shook? Why can't I move my feet? Why ain't these lot takin' note of this guy? He's coming closer. I can't…

(*Frightened*.) *'We… we should come off this bridge.'*

Did that even come out? It ricocheted in my head but I bet it didn't come. I feel warm piss run down the inside of my leg.

Baker finds a new stone.

'Ahh what? That's too big!' says Jerome.

'How's it too big?'

'That's a fucking boulder.'

'But go on, I bet you still miss.'

'I'm gonna get it in its face.'

(*Closes his eyes*.)

I wish this guy would disappear. I wish this guy would disappear.

(*Opens his eyes, looks*.)

Wait. I recognise his face.

'Come here, little baby.'

'Nar nar nar, that's cheating, bruv, you can't make the baby come to you, drop it now or the bet's off.'

'Blesssss blesssss blesssss.'

(*Baker drops the rock*.)

(*Long beat*.)

Taruvangadum. It was Mr Taruvangadum. He rushed over with a quickness.

'Sir sir, we found a baby,' said Baker.

'We found a baby, sir,' said Jerome.

'Yo, Rugrat... Rugrat, are you crying, bruv?'

We get to some church where everybody's been waiting for us. The CRB Youngers were there, Terence and dat. We're greeted with a loud cheer that echoes bad. I could hear Babatunde's overloud clap, distorting. Feel like a prodigal son, except I don't want the praise. I got the phattest weight on my chest pinning me down.

Baker's a hero. For finding the baby. He's smiling big. Fucking yellow teeth. The teachers rub his head. He's a fucking nobleman, a crown prince.

'Ah was the one that saw it, innit, they didn't even believe me,' he said.

This guy. Felt like telling him to shut his mouth. Instead I walked up to him and punched him in the face. Twice. They all thought I was crazy. Felt so good though, man. The second punch didn't even connect properly, I think I caught his neck or something but it felt good.

Something weird come over me that day. Had an out-of-body experience. I woke up. I could see where I was in life, and I could distinguish between where I was heading and where I wanted to be. I grew up. We don't grow up on our birthdays, it's on random experiences like this one.

Joanne

Thing is. Nobody saw him but me. No one saw him but me so when I'm telling them he left. I look mad, innit. I sound mental. I'm flippin' out though. Fighting his corner, he's my boy, innit. I'm blowing up. About I'm chatting shit –

'He was here so shut – YES HE *WAS* HERE, close your breath or you're gonna feel a – '

(JOANNE *suddenly lashes out at someone*.)

I have to break Frankie's arm cos she don't believe me. People don't understand though. They all thought I was crazy. I'm jumping round like Ali now. Whoever wants some –

'Cooome. Come, bredrin!'

(*She skips and jumps around in a boxer's stance.*

The CHORUS *slowly close in on her. She puts up a fight but they manage to hold her arms down*.)

This was when I fell to pieces. And this was when more doctors than I knew even existed began trying to piece me back together again.

I ain't crazy.

I'm just hurt.

But try telling them that when you've got half an umbilical cord hanging out of you with no baby to show. Real talk.

He's out there in the world somewhere. It's the magnets. I can feel him still.

He may have disappeared but you know what? The boy never leaves.

(*She touches the back of her neck like* KEHINDE *did, she smiles as they spin her away.*)

EPILOGUE

RUGRAT. As the world gets better at spinning!

JOANNE. We get dizzy and fall on our rare.

KEHINDE. Some keep falling through the atmosphere.

RUGRAT. Some don't survive past 12:05.

KEHINDE. But if you've got *this* – (*Heart.*)

JOANNE. And if you use *this* – (*Brains.*)

RUGRAT. And if you're not afraid of being you.

KEHINDE. If most of what you say is what you do.

JOANNE. Then everyfing is gonna be cool.

RUGRAT. Don't forget your dreams –

KEHINDE. – Dreams that are forgotten do not blossom.

JOANNE. Live, but don't run too fast.

RUGRAT. Play, but don't forget to read.

KEHINDE. Focus, but don't forget to eat.

JOANNE. Love, but keep your nobility – real talk.

RUGRAT. Study, but don't forget to learn.

KEHINDE. Be knowledgeable, but don't forget to listen.

JOANNE. Seek, but don't forget your vision.

RUGRAT. Travel, but be at home with yourself.

ALL. BE YOUNG!

JOANNE. – Be young, you can't forget to be young, so be young, but don't forget to grow –

RUGRAT. – Oh no –

JOANNE. – You gotta grow.

KEHINDE. And strive, but only with self-respect.

JOANNE. When happy see the virtue in sadness.

RUGRAT. When crowded appreciate the peacefulness of loneliness.

KEHINDE. When rich find the hunger poverty-generated.

JOANNE. Aspire, but don't forget to be.

RUGRAT. Aspire, but don't forget to be.

KEHINDE. Aspire, but don't forget to be.

(*Lights to black.*)

A Nick Hern Book

Little Baby Jesus first published in Great Britain in 2011 as a paperback original by Nick Hern Books Limited, The Glasshouse, 49a Goldhawk Road, London W12 8QP, in association with the Oval House Theatre, London

Reprinted 2012

Little Baby Jesus copyright © 2011 Arinze Kene

Arinze Kene has asserted his right to be identified as the author of this work

Cover image: weareasilia.com
Cover design: Ned Hoste, 2H

Typeset by Nick Hern Books, London
Printed in the UK by Mimeo Ltd, Huntingdon, Cambridgeshire PE29 6XX

A CIP catalogue record for this book is available from the British Library

ISBN 978 1 84842 199 8

Woodland
CARBON
www.woodlandcarbon.co.uk
NICK HERN BOOKS
Printed on Carbon Captured paper